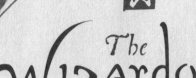

The Wizardology™ Handbook

A Course for Apprentices

Being a True *Account* of *Wizards*,

Their *Ways* and Many Wonderful *Powers*
as told by ⟨Master⟩ ⟨Merlin⟩.

Printed by *L.P.* for
The Templar Company.

Edited for the modern *Reader* by
Dugald A. Steer

By Most Special *Order*. MDLXXVII

As Above, So Below

```
        A
       A B
      A B R
     A B R A
    A B R A C
   A B R A C A
  A B R A C A D
 A B R A C A D A
A B R A C A D A B
A B R A C A D A B R
A B R A C A D A B R A
```

To assist the growth of
magical herbs and plants
write the word above on
a piece of parchment and
plant it with their seeds.
Otherwise, wrap it around
the stem. As the word
doth grow, so mote
the plant.

While learning the art of dowsing for magical treasure, the forgetful apprentice may consider it worth making two dowsing rods, so that if the first is mislaid or lost, it may be possible to relocate it using the second. If both become lost, give up dowsing.

First published in the *UK* in 2006 by *TEMPLAR PUBLISHING*,
an imprint of *The Templar Company Plc*,
Pippbrook Mill, London Road, Dorking, Surrey, RH4 1JE, UK

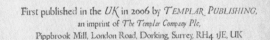

Illustration Copyright © 2006 John Howe,
Anne Yvonne Gilbert, Tomislav Tomic and Helen Ward.
Text and Design Copyright © 2006 The Templar Company Plc.
Wizardology™ is a trademark of The Templar Company Plc.
Designed by *Jonathan Lambert* and *Nghiem Ta*.

Publisher's Note: Over the *Centuries* a *Number* of *Books* have laid *Claim* to having been penned by a certain *Wizard* named *Master Merlin*, but few have dared to provide true *Instruction* for wizardological *Apprentices*. The *Publisher* does not recommend meddling in magical *Matters*, and cautions those who do so only to attempt *Spells* for the *Good* of *Others*.

templar publishing

www.wizardology.com

ꓨ ꙲꙲꙲꙲ O꙲꙲꙲꙲꙲꙲꙲꙲ ꙲꙲꙲ ꙲꙲꙲꙲꙲ ꙲꙲꙲ ꙲꙲꙲
꙲OO꙲꙲ ꙲꙲O ꙲꙲꙲꙲꙲꙲O꙲꙲ ꙲꙲꙲꙲꙲

CONTENTS

A heartfelt *plea* to all
SELFISH APPRENTICES
to put away this *book* and forget *wizardology,*
for the *world* may be in much greater *need* of *scientists.*

HOSE WHO STUDY the art of wizardology must remember that all magic is an act of the imagination. Helpful, positive thoughts aimed at assisting others may bring helpful, positive results. Unhelpful, negative thoughts are more likely to rebound on the sender due to a powerful magical law known as the Rule of Three. This rule states that negative magic will rebound on the sender with three times more force than it was sent out. An apprentice should be careful what he imagines magically. He must also remember that some acts of imagination are more difficult than others. I, for example, have great trouble imagining that the usual run-of-the-mill apprentice stands any chance of becoming a great wizard. My familiars Harpier, Greymalkin and Paddock—the kindly animals who have become my wizardological companions—agree with me. They disappeared the minute I magically told them of my plan to turn the tree where I had been imprisoned into a book in order to seek out an apprentice worthy to be my magical successor. They felt that the most likely result of my labours would be that anyone laying their hands on my book would start trying to use it for negative, selfish ends. I told them that, while modern apprentices might be stupid, at least they would not be so greedy or downright wicked as they were in the old days. My familiars did not believe me.

Luckily, Harpier, my most faithful familiar, recanted. He agreed to provide assistance and I am writing this book in order to fulfil a promise to him that I would provide a new

Gladde

Pranxtor

Jaypes

Larfor

Magic is not a serious matter. It should be made with a light heart in order to work properly. In this book, each of the elements and seasons is associated with a playful spirit. To summon them, imagine their symbol glowing. Their names are: Gladde, spirit of Water and Spring, who helps with creative magic; Pranxtor, spirit of Fire and Summer, useful in works of strength; Jaypes, spirit of Air and Autumn, who helps bring wisdom; and Larfor, spirit of Earth and Winter, useful in assisting with remarkable and often amusing changes.

book of magical instruction with the natural world of the elements and seasons as its basis. There were a few pieces of trunk left after I created my last book, after all. And who knows? Maybe there will be *one* apprentice who will make use of my book to make positive magic. To all others I say: give up wizardology. It will certainly go awry unless you use it positively. The spirits are tired of running after mean, selfish masters. It may well be that there is greater need of scientists than old-fashioned wonder-workers. I recommend that you attend one of those new-fangled "schools" and see if you can find out.

AS I WILL, SO MOTE IT BE!

Anno Domini 1577

My familiars are unamused by those who try to use my magic selfishly.

GABL

During the spring, magical plants begin to grow. Tongue of Dog, or Hound's Tongue, only reaches its full power during the Summer.

Eye of Newt, *also known as the Daisy, is at its most powerful during the Spring Equinox and on mid-summer's day.*

Although the phoenix is often associated with the element of fire, its regenerative abilities make feathers from a young phoenix useful in Spring magic. Likewise, unicorn horn can also be a powerful ingredient if dipped in potions.

Water

∇

SPRING

Spring is the ideal time for beginnings and making a new start. Now is the time when the would-be wizard should plan to work with each of the four wizardly paths: of western wizards, eastern sages, chinese masters and shamans. Special attention should be paid to how nature blooms into life. Spells involving water should be performed, and old friendships renewed. Now is the time to plan out the magical year ahead.

Hail Gladde, the serious spirit of Spring, crying:

GATKA ATGA,
BUDS IN MAY.
SPRING IS SPRUNG,
IT'S TIME TO PLAY.

Gladde

WESTERN WIZARDS

Descendants of an ancient order, wizards must remember that power and responsibility go hand in hand.

HE PATH OF THE WESTERN WIZARD is fraught with many dangers. Greatest of these, perhaps, is the likelihood that the would-be wizard will decide, after learning one or two simple spells and charms, that he is now a powerful magus and will seek to impress his friends with his new abilities, forgetting that ill-used magic has a tendency to backfire in a highly amusing fashion. Some wizards who lack imagination simply repeat spells they have learned by rote and never learn their own. However, there is a practical and very simple remedy that may be applied for all of these errors: giving up magic altogether.

ഔ ANCIENT WAYS ൙

The lore of Western wizards has come from many different sources. The most important of these is the ancient lore of the druids. Contrary to popular belief, not all of the druids were destroyed in their Welsh strongholds by Roman invaders. Instead, many of them survived as bards and wizards, keeping their knowledge of the old ways alive and passing them on to their pupils, who henceforth became known as wizardological apprentices. The poetry of the ancient druids has also survived in many forms, not only in their rhyming spells, but also in their prophetic sayings, as has their great and enduring love of the natural world and of creatures of all kinds.

Things Common to Western Wizards :

Dwellings: A hermit's cell deep in a forest, a ruined tower. *Habits*: Using and charging magical items, working with fairies and sprites. *Length of Study*: Ten years. *Weaknesses*: Some spend too much time studying science, others become petty conjurors. *Usual Payment*: Gold, or better, goodwill and a good deed done in return.

Western wizards are constantly pursued by people seeking to have their wishes granted. I have created a simple wishing spell, which ought to work and so save a lot of bother.

◦◦ *WISHING SPELL* ◦◦

Look up at the moon, holding a piece of magic mistletoe in one hand and a phoenix feather in the other. Imagine the sun rising and your wish being granted as you say the following words:

✳

I have a wish I wish I had,
Larfor, Pranxtor, Jaypes and Gladde.
Wish with me, I'll wish with you,
And make my wishing words come true.
My wishing words are:
PHOENIXMISTLE!
MISTLEPHOENIX!

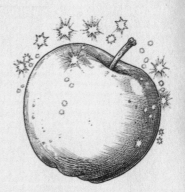

With a few changes, the spell can be used to make an ordinary apple into a wishing one. If it does not work, then at least the natural magical powers of the apple will continue to render visits to a doctor less likely.

WIZARD EQUIPMENT

Apprentices must remember they do not need every item of equipment shown here in order to work magic. But they should know what these things represent. A SPELL BOOK represents the wizard's store of magical knowledge; a CRYSTAL BALL his wisdom in predicting the likely outcome of events; a TOAD his understanding of nature; a CAULDRON his wizardological power and the WANDS the means to direct that magic appropriately.

Spell book

Crystal ball

Cauldron

Magic wands

Toad

If You Meet a Western Wizard
DO...

* Be very polite indeed
* Explain that you are a student of wizardology
* Say how handsome his owl familiar looks today
* Wish him both good day and good luck
* Leave him to go about his business in peace

If You Meet a Western Wizard
DO NOT...

* Challenge him to a magical duel involving wands
* Frighten his familiars
* Cross his palm with silver
* Offer to stir his cauldron for a year and a day
* Pull on his long beard
* Jump up and down on his hat
* Ask him to grant you wishes

❧ WITCHES ❧

Good witches show that you do not need expensive equipment in order to make magic. Their means of flight doubles as a way of cleaning the floor. Their means of brewing potions doubles as a cooking pot. So never accept food from a witch—even a good one—in case she has not had time to clean her cauldron properly.

The Way of a Western Wizard :

If you choose to follow the way of the Western wizard here is the path to take. Firstly, you will spend several years finding a master. These years can be usefully spent reading books such as this one. When you find a master, you will spend eight years stirring his cauldron, laundering his robes and looking after his familiars. Unless you are lucky, he or she will not teach you any magic at all. After this, your master may allow you to perform the odd spell, but mainly in order to enjoy your discomfort when things go wrong. If you survive this ordeal without becoming a toad or growing a donkey's ears, your master will at last consider you fit to learn the secrets of wizardology although, had you been listening, you could have learnt them from his owl familiar all along.

WIZARD WORK : An apprentice wizard ought to be inspired by stories of great wizards from the past. He should find a book about King Arthur in a bookshop or library, and read about how I managed to help that mighty king from so long ago.

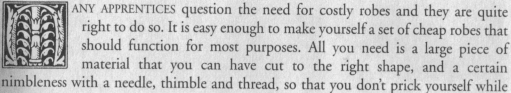

Lesson II :

A WIZARD'S ROBES

Any *apprentice* who is at all serious about their.
wizardly *work* must create a proper *set* of magical *robes.*

MANY APPRENTICES question the need for costly robes and they are quite right to do so. It is easy enough to make yourself a set of cheap robes that should function for most purposes. All you need is a large piece of material that you can have cut to the right shape, and a certain nimbleness with a needle, thimble and thread, so that you don't prick yourself while sewing the robes. When they are finished, you should only wear the robes for wizardological work—such as reading this book or casting spells. The spell below should help to make sure that the robes also give a modicum of magical protection.

Decorating the Robes :

Some question why a wizard needs to wear robes at all. As with all items of magical equipment, they help to make your magic work by allowing you to feel that you are a proper wizard—even if you are merely a bumbling beginner. They can be decorated with symbols and letters as appropriate.

$0 *THE ROBE SPELL* $0

Touch your new robe with silver on a Monday, then sprinkle it with fresh rainwater as you recite the following charm seven times:

✳

*Spirits of Earth and Air,
I call on you to vow
Spirits of Fire and Water,
My robe protects me now.*
*VESTIMENT FORTIS!
FORTIS MAGICO!*

✳

APPRENTICE ROBE

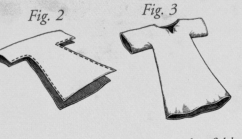

Fig. 1   Fig. 2   Fig. 3   Fig. 4

Figs. 2 & 3: The material is folded in half, and a piece is cut out to allow the wizard's head to poke through.

Fig. 1: A piece of cloth one-and-a-half times the wizard's height is cut out according to the correct pattern.

Fig. 4: The robe is sewn neatly on each side along the edges and across the bottom of each sleeve. It is then decorated. A belt will finish off the robe nicely.

Choosing a Hat :

When it comes to wizardology, the hat makes the wizard, so choose wisely, or make your own hat from stiff cloth or velvet. In extreme circumstances, a paper hat will do.

SYMBOLS AND THEIR MEANINGS *to adorn your robes*

Moon   Mars   Mercury   Sun   Venus   Jupiter   Saturn   Air   Earth   Fire   Water

Further alchemical symbols can be found on page 31.

Further alchemical symbols can be found on page 31.

WIZARD WORK : The apprentice should make his own set of robes using the instructions above, and find a suitable hat. If this is not possible, a large conical hat can be made from paper, decorated with appropriate magical letters and symbols.

Lesson III:

FAIRIES & ELVES

As it is *fairies* and *elves* who help us to perform our magic, a word or two about them might be useful.

LWAYS REMEMBER that it is invisible fairies and elves who work the apparently magical effects of our spells and charms. Their classification into undines, sylphs, gnomes and so forth is not exact, for these spirits go by many different names in different parts of the world—leprechauns and clurichauns, boggarts, wee men, hadas, to name but few. It is the nature of the spells we use that attract one or more of these spirits and make them perform our work, and it must always be remembered that they are unlikely to be doing so willingly.

Fairies may be found in threes near old monuments such as standing stones. Here they wait to enforce the RULE OF THREE on foolish wizards who have worked wicked magic there, for wicked magic returns on its caster *threefold*.

While some sprites adopt large or sinister forms, these are never their true appearance.

Spellcaster Beware : Should a fairy ever appear to you—particularly during a spellcasting session—be very careful. It is sure to promise you all sorts of things, but unless you are performing the spell exactly, repeating the words without any mistakes, and only doing magic for the benefit of others, then it is sure to be trying to deceive you.

ELF CHARM

This spell is useful when making decisions. It calls on fairies to help you as you decide what to do. Cast a little salt as you walk around the inside of a mushroom fairy ring, then bow, crying:

*

Fairy folk of marsh and heath,
Fairy folk of wood and hill,
Fairy folk above, beneath,
Fairies moving, fairies still,
I take a bow,
So help me now.

*

Background: merry Larfor. Front left: laughing Jaypes. Right: Gladde. Pranxtor is always invisible.

Fairy Rings :

Circles in the woods made from rings of toadstools provide natural magical protection. They are a particularly useful place for making important decisions, as the wizard will find himself beyond the influence of external forces. Remember that on no account should any of the mushrooms be eaten as they may be poisonous.

WIZARD WORK : The apprentice should try to find out about local fairy legends. If he has a garden, he should proceed to the bottom of it in the early morning and search under bushes—preferably gooseberry bushes—for signs of fairy activity.

WIZARD FAMILIARS

Animals are a *wizard's* true *friends*, for they
can teach him more than even the mightiest *master*.

ESTERN WIZARDS ARE well known for their love of the natural world. In order to understand this world as fully as possible, they often work with animals called familiars, who are able to see the fairies and sprites they are working with. These animals may, to all intents and purposes, appear to be pets and the wizard must make sure to take good care of them. There is another class of familiars, however, that normally goes unseen by ordinary human sight. This is the class of magical animals. Of particular importance, especially for female wizards, is the unicorn.

Summoning a Unicorn Familiar :

Proceed to a source of water in an outdoor or woodland location, as this gives you the best chance of locating unicorns. Should you be lucky enough to find one, he will accompany you in invisible form. It is best not to tell any non-wizards about your invisible familiar, as they are likely to think you are mad.

⁸⁰ UNICORN SPELL ˢ°

To try to summon a unicorn, find a clear pool of water in a natural location. Gaze at your own reflection in the pool as you recite the following spell. Bray three times loudly. If successful, you will soon see the unicorn appear beside you.

✳

Unicorns, unicorns all around,
Waiting near water, there to be found,
Lions are distant, none are found here,
Unicorn, unicorn, swiftly appear.
Horses may neigh, but I will now bray,
And when I bray, you'll come here today!

✳

LIBER ZOOLOGICUM

This ancient tome—the LIBER ZOOLOGICUM lists some useful names of animals that can be used in magic when you find a familiar. Be careful to conceal this name, especially from foolish so-called Witch Finders, like Matthew Hopkins, who thought you could tell a witch by identifying her familiars. This did not work, for the real familiars would be sure to vanish, or assume the forms of ordinary-looking pets as soon as he turned up.

On the right is a selection of magical creatures: Vinegar Tom the cat is renowned for his magical mousing abilities. Harpier the owl has great sense and wisdom. Sacke-and-Sugar the toad has a knack of infiltrating marshes. Pyewacket the hare possesses extreme hearing skills. Grizzle Greedigut the dog has an amazing technique of making things vanish— particularly food.

WIZARD WORK : Young apprentices should make a habit of studying some local animals. Even cities are not entirely destitute of creatures such as birds, squirrels or foxes. A chart can be constructed showing what the animal does, and at what times, which is useful later should the animal need your care.

Lesson V:
Harpier's Lore:
WEATHER MAGIC

Whether the *weather* be hot or cold, wet or dry,
it has a profound *effect* on our ability to work *magic*.

WEATHER AND THE SEASONS ought to be as important to wizards as they are to owls. Trying to perform a spell at the wrong time of year, or during the wrong kind of weather, only makes things difficult, like trying to fly with lead weights on your wings. It is natural that there are more water spirits about when it is raining, and that any seen in dry weather are likely to be found near water. While there are general rules, each wizard must study the weather and seasons himself in order to develop a proper understanding of the subject.

RAIN SPELL

This is the most common type of spell that wizards are called upon to perform. To cast the spell sprinkle nine drops of water on dry earth: three of dew, three from a sea or lake, and three raindrops. Say the following spell as you imagine lots of rain falling down:

*

Nine drops by nine are eighty-one,
Eighty-one clouds shall bring me rain,
The rain shall fall, the land shall smile,
And water flow for a long while.

*

Types of Magic to Perform Under Certain Weather Conditions :
Rain spells are best cast during extremely dry spells. Wind spells are best cast when a sailor finds himself becalmed. Otherwise, the wizard should avoid interfering with the natural processes of nature.

On the Times of the Day :
Spells relating to beginnings are best confined to the early morning. Spells involving divination or those that are designed to affect a person are best cast in the evening or late afternoon. Flying spells are best cast at midday.

Monday	Friday
Tuesday	Saturday
Wednesday	Sunday
Thursday	

On the Season of the Year :

The seasons are related to the four magical elements: Earth, Air, Fire and Water. A good wizard pays attention to these. Answers to questions are best sought in Autumn. Spring spells often involve friendship. Winter is a time for spells involving health or finding lost treasure. Summer is an excellent time for spells of good luck and prosperity.

On the Phases of the Moon :

Fairies and sprites live their lives according to the phases of the Moon. As such, it is a powerful aid to magic. The New Moon is a time for creation, the Waxing Moon a time for increasing power, the Full Moon a time for completion, while the Waning Moon is a time of change. As the nights are darker, so is the magic brighter.

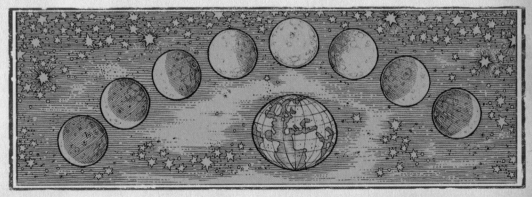

WIZARD WORK : An apprentice should keep a weather record suitable to the area in which he lives. This should also record important seasonal events such as when the first snowdrops are seen, when the first cuckoo is heard and when the first leaf falls.

TALES OF FAIRY GOLD

Non-magical *dealings* with *fairies* and *elves* are usually fraught with *danger*—be on your *guard* at all *times*.

THERE ARE MANY STORIES involving fairies and elves that should act as cautionary tales for the would-be wizard. Although these creatures mostly hide themselves from human sight, there are times when they can appear—often at dusk or twilight, or on special days of the year such as midwinter or around the equinoxes. Without wizard ways to control them, they can be tricky customers, but this difficult behaviour tends only to arise when the person seeing them starts to expect three wishes, or gold.

Stories about the Irish sprites are particularly instructive, as that island has a magical atmosphere which means appearances are rather more frequent than in other places. One such sprite is the leprechaun. This sprite is most often found under a hedge in the guise of a cobbler, mending a single shoe. Magically, you must not take even one eye off a leprechaun if you should see one, because that will give him the chance to disappear, which he is quite sure to do.

One cautionary tale involving a leprechaun involves a man and woman who came across one by chance. Knowing that leprechauns are supposed to have a magical crock of gold, the couple, without taking their eyes off him, took a hold of him and demanded to know its whereabouts before they would let him go. The wily leprechaun answered that he would gladly tell them.

It was raining, and all they had to do was follow the rainbow which they could see in the sky to the end, and there they would find the coveted crock. Of couse, even non-wizards know that a rainbow is an illusion created by the action of sunlight passing through raindrops, so it is clear that a rainbow actually has no end that can be reached—it simply seems to get farther away the closer you get to it. And so it is more likely than not that the foolish couple are still seeking the leprechaun's gold to this very day.

Another thing to remember about leprechauns is that they are good at spells involving illusion. If one gives you some gold or silver coins you must be careful to use a spell that will reverse the illusion immediately. Otherwise you will suffer disappointment when what you thought were shiny gold coins turn to nothing more than leaves as soon as the leprechaun has gone.

Be very careful if the leprechaun suggests that he will grant you three wishes instead of giving you gold. This is a common trick because, to a leprechaun, granting wishes merely means allowing you to wish for things. Actually making sure that those things come to pass is not usually part of the bargain.

The would-be wizard must be very careful how he speaks to an elf in such an encounter, or he is likely to lose more than his shirt. While your life may not be in danger, there is a very good chance that your pride or health could suffer if you make the wrong choices.

Eye of Newt

Midsummer's Day, the 21st
June, is a most excellent
time for collecting all sorts
of magical herbs and plants
for our spells.

Adder's Fork

Toe of Frog

FEETWEAR FOR WIZARDS

Amazing
SEVEN LEAGUE BOOTS

Any Size, Any Colour
M. Winklepicker Esq., Cobbler,
Leatherhead, England

PARACELSUS

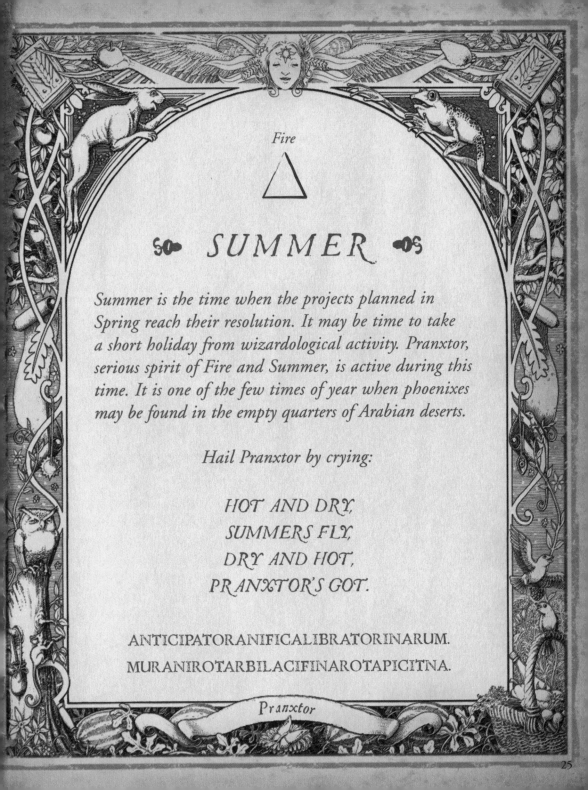

Fire

△

SUMMER

Summer is the time when the projects planned in Spring reach their resolution. It may be time to take a short holiday from wizardological activity. Pranxtor, serious spirit of Fire and Summer, is active during this time. It is one of the few times of year when phoenixes may be found in the empty quarters of Arabian deserts.

Hail Pranxtor by crying:

HOT AND DRY,
SUMMERS FLY,
DRY AND HOT,
PRANXTOR'S GOT.

ANTICIPATORANIFICALIBRATORINARUM.
MURANIROTARBILACIFINAROTAPICITNA.

Pranxtor

Lesson VII:

SAGES OF ARABIA

*That the true lamp of learning was kept alight
by a handful of wise sages is much to be wondered at.*

 NLIKE WESTERN WIZARDS, who tend to rely on master/apprentice teaching for their learning, the sages of Arabia, Persia and North Africa rely on the wisdom of the ancient masters as presented in their books. Of course, books were largely unavailable during the so-called Dark Ages in Europe, and so it was the Arabian sages who carried on the tradition of magical learning laid down by the Romans, Greeks and Ancient Egyptians. A requisite for any apprentice who wishes to follow this path is a profound love of books, and a desire to work with codes and other methods of hiding secret information.

ॐ LEARNING ॐ

One side effect of the Arabian sages' love of learning is their tendency to drop proper wizardological pursuits in favour of history, geography, mathematics, alchemy and other highly unsuitable topics. Luckily, a few of them manage to overcome this danger and find themselves working with genies in the proper spirit of wizardology, and paying no heed to scientific experiments, or other things that might weaken their belief in the magic that they weave. A trip on a magical carpet, or an encounter with a particularly wise or old genie is usually enough to put stragglers back on the right track, but some are still stubborn enough to go on working in ways in which no true wizard could ever really approve.

Things Common to Arabian Sages :

Dwellings: A house with a laboratory attached, often in a city. *Habits*: Creators and collectors of magical items such as flying carpets and old books. Dealing with genies. *Length of Study*: A lifetime. *Weaknesses*: For some, the desire for scientific knowledge can be too strong to resist. *Usual Payment*: Knowledge, or an item of magical value.

Anyone wishing to follow the example of the Arabian sages needs to begin to build up a collection of amazing magical items as soon as possible, or to start creating their own using simple spells and charms.

❧ HEALTH SPELL ❧

This spell assists cures by charming a genie into a yellow apple. Unfortunately, it is easy to mispronounce the words and, if this happens, the apple is more likely to cause indigestion than any miraculous healing effects.

*

Yellow djinn with opal eyes,
I call thee by thy proper name,
And to this apple in my hand,
I bind thee to the same!

AVLARꟻ AVLARꟻ
AVLARꟻ KEBIR
ALMI MA-A UBLU

*

Apple of Healing

Spyglass of Revealing

The Dangerous Entrapment of Genies:

GENIES—WHO ARE also known as djinn—are not difficult to trap. They can take a variety of forms, but most often prefer to appear in human shape. As they are denizens of hot countries, the sudden application of cold can often make them appear visible. The process below is given for information only—it is forbidden to trap any creature.

Note that the process for trapping a genie in a door, to prevent unauthorised entry is basically the same as in the spell below, only the words, "Close Sesame" replace the words, "Jayeed Jayeed" in the spell.

Force any djinn to become visible by cooling the room down with several large lumps of ice. Quickly produce the lamp before the genie can escape.

GENIE SPELL
Perform according to the instructions and following the pictures on the left.

*

By ice I detect you,
My mind shows my need,
Look into my eyes
Obey me in deed!
HATHA KA-AFI
JAYEED JAYEED

*

Repeat the spell seven times, imagining the genie being drawn into the lamp. Cap the lamp. The genie inside can be released by rubbing the lamp anticlockwise seven times.

GEBER

Apprentices should note the path of the alchemist Geber, the 8th-century Arabian "father of chemistry". Instead of following the path of wizardology, he declared that the only way to gain true knowledge was through a great deal of practical work and experimentation. His works include notes on scientific procedures such as distillation, crystallisation and evaporation. While no doubt interesting, performing experiments is likely to be a distraction from true magical practice. But learning is to be encouraged.

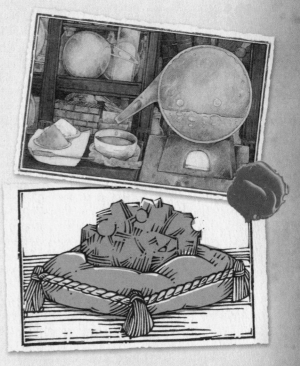

Alembics :

A true wizard would be unlikely to use anything as cumbersome as an alembic to separate various parts of a liquid through evaporation. He would more likely use magic to get some helpful spirits to do it for him.

The Philosopher's Stone :

The idea that there is a stone that can help purify other materials persists. It may be that a wizard charmed a lump of rock with curative properties and an early alchemist believed it to have been a natural phenomena.

WIZARD WORK : The apprentice should seek out a copy of *The Thousand and One Nights* and read it. He should search for old lamps or bottles, and release any trapped genies, using two wishes to help others and one to protect the genie.

Lesson VIII :

A WIZARD'S WAND

Without a *means* to focus magical *force*, the
wizard's mastery of even simple *spells* will be in *vain*.

HE APPRENTICE MUST take proper care of all of his wands. They
should be wrapped up in a piece of cloth when not in use. Below
you can see some examples of wands.

They can be
constructed
according to the chart on
page 64 of this book, or
according to any other
system that the apprentice
prefers. Staffs can likewise
be made, although a staff
ought to be decorated with
either no symbols at all, or
with a range of symbols,
given that a staff can be
used to perform a wide
variety of magic. They are
not, however, as specialised
as wands.

Fig. 1 Wand of Friendship
Of green olive wood, tipped with a copper dove and emerald

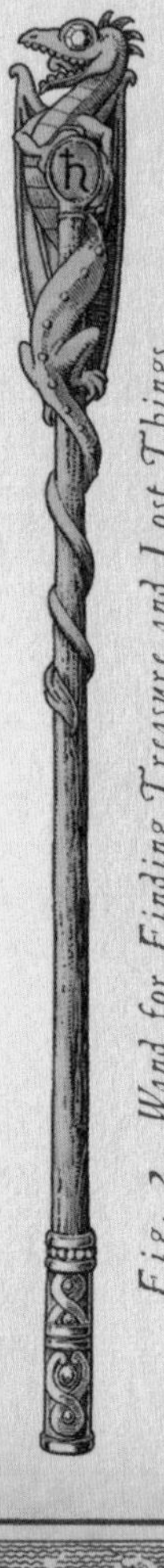

Fig. 2 Wand for Finding Treasure and Lost Things
Of yew, pewter based, tipped with a violet dragon and diamond

Fig. 3 Wand for Understanding Difficult Things
Of hazel, entwined with serpents, tipped with owl's wings and opal

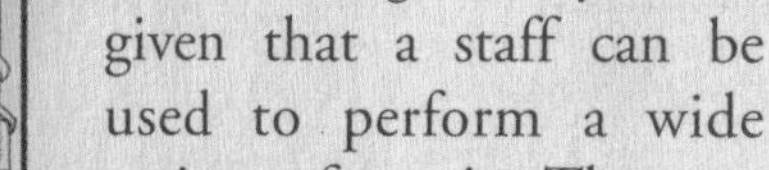

*There are many tales of apprentices
hurting themselves using a wizard's
knife, or athame. ALWAYS ask an
older person to do any cutting for
you. It will never affect the magic.*

⊷ THE WAND SPELL ⊶

Dip your wand in a stream of running water on the
night of a New Moon. Wave it seven times and
imagine a flame, a breath of air, a raindrop and a
shower of sand pouring into your wand as you cry:

✳

I thank the tree that gave me thee,
This wizard power now works for me!

✳

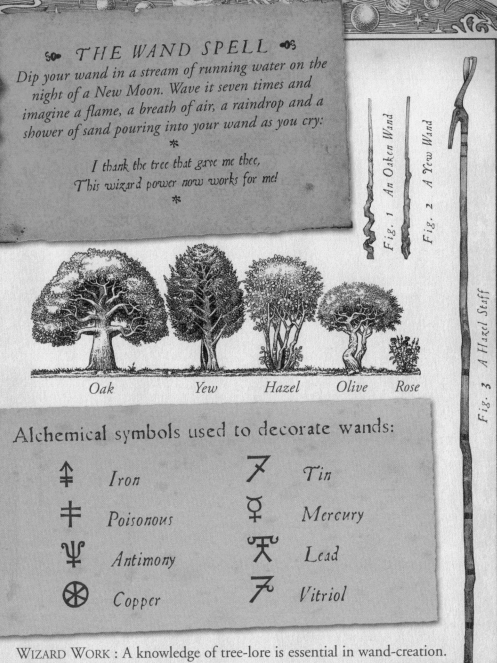

Fig. 1 An Oaken Wand

Fig. 2 A Yew Wand

Fig. 3 A Hazel Staff

Oak   Yew   Hazel   Olive   Rose

Alchemical symbols used to decorate wands:

⚧	Iron	♉	Tin
⚰	Poisonous	☿	Mercury
♆	Antimony	♄	Lead
⊕	Copper	⚡	Vitriol

WIZARD WORK : A knowledge of tree-lore is essential in wand-creation.
The apprentice should seek out someone who knows about trees, or read
about them in a book, learning all he can.

Lesson IX:

WIZARDS' CODES

As *wizardology* must be kept secret, so *wizards*
have devised various secret *means* of communication.

*Foolish Dr. Faustus made a
pact with Mephistopheles.
Read the words around his
magic circle using the
Sigillum Mysteriorum.*

 F COURSE, MOST WIZARDS are more than happy to use simpler forms of communication over distances than codes, which can be easily broken. But, for wizards who wish to communicate not only through space but also through time, codes have become a very important part of their magical repertoire and are a very serious subject of study. The apprentice will be rewarded if he pays attention to how some traditional codes are formed, and how he may create his own.

Substitution Cyphers :

The simplest form of code is known as the substitution cypher. In this code, other letters or symbols are substituted for the letters of the alphabet, so that an A may become a B, for example, a B a C and so forth. Ep Zpv Voefstuboe? The Sigillum Mysteriorum shown on the next page is another example of this type of code.

Other Codes :

Codes obviously demand extreme secrecy. Codes can either be made from the first letters of each word Or by Demonstrating skill in Emphasising certain letters in a sentence Simply by placing them in capitals. Other codes use numbers to identify letters in a paragraph such as this one. If fish delights you: 1, 6, 15, 44, 65, 100, 173, 179, 180.

Codes Used for Making Predictions :

Some wizards, such as the notorious Nostradamus, seem to delight in making all sorts of dire predictions about future events. Sometimes these predictions are written in code. The parchment on the next page was supposedly found among the effects of the Elizabethan magus Dr. Dee and refers to an event that is to happen in 1896.

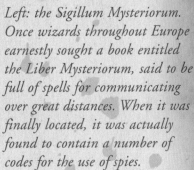

Left: the Sigillum Mysteriorum. Once wizards throughout Europe earnestly sought a book entitled the Liber Mysteriorum, said to be full of spells for communicating over great distances. When it was finally located, it was actually found to contain a number of codes for the use of spies.

WIZARD WORK : The apprentice should practise making codes by devising one based on a chapter from a book owned by both him and a friend. Identify the letters by numbers e.g. 1 is the first letter, 2 the second etc. Unless they know the book, no one can decipher the code. Make sure that both use exactly the same version of the book. In this paragraph: 12, 14, 17, 30, 35, 37, 76, 78, 131, 150, 151, 160.

DEAL WITH GENIES

Refuse a *genie's* offer of three *wishes* when you release *him* and you may well make a useful and powerful *ally*.

HE PROBLEM WITH genies, as with other fairies and elves, is that there is very little that we can offer them—apart from occasionally their freedom—that they either need or want. This is why we must use spells to cause them to do our bidding, and why they are rightly wary of human beings, particularly those dressed up in magical robes. Therefore, unless you visit the remoter parts of the Arabian desert, the most likely time that you will come across a genie is when you find a lamp or bottle in which one has been imprisoned. As the genie will be furious, special care must be taken to release them properly.

Bottle

Lamp

Chamber pot

How to Release a Genie Safely :

* Imagine the symbols for Gladde, Jaypes, Larfor and Pranxtor glowing around you, or draw them on pieces of card.
* Prepare some ice and a new jar or bottle, and get ready to use the Genie Spell on page 28 if all goes wrong.
* Rub the jar, lamp or bottle seven times widdershins (i.e. anticlockwise).
* Stand well back.
* Don't ask for difficult wishes.
* A quick method is just to smash the jar or bottle with a long pole or stick.
NOTE: Some wizards have been known to hurl clay bottles or lamps containing angry genies among their enemies.

WIZARD WORK : The apprentice should use an atlas to find the mountain called Jebel Toubkal in the country of Morocco. He should plan an expedition to seek out the local genies and write a report of what he expects to find out.

Harpier's Lore: PLANT MAGIC

Most things written about plant *magic* are *nonsense*.
The *apprentice* is advised to study this *topic* for himself.

T IS A LITTLE-KNOWN FACT that four of the most commonly used magical plants each have a relation to one of the seasons, and so also to one of the four spirits, Gladde, Jaypes, Larfor and Pranxtor. As such, they can be used in magic relating to these spirits, who may be attracted to areas where these plants bloom in profusion. Interestingly, the time that a plant is in bloom does not necessarily relate to the season with which it is associated.

Working with Magical Plants :

The apprentice will no doubt be able to construct their own spells according to the instructions on page 64. Remember, spells should not involve eating any of the plants, as this tends to destroy rather than augment their magical force. Many plants can be used in magic. The way to determine their magical properties is detailed opposite.

Eye of Newt, *or the Daisy, is magically linked with Air, Jaypes and Autumn. Plants collected on Midsummer's Day may be used in spells involving divination. To call Jaypes, wear a bangle made from a chain of* Eye of Newt *flowers.*

Adder's Fork, *or Adder's Tongue, is associated with Earth, Larfor and Winter. To call Larfor, merely stand near one of these plants, holding a piece of clay or clod of earth in each gloved hand.*

Tongue of Dog, or Hound's Tongue, is associated with Water, Gladde and Spring. Dip flowers of this plant into water to call Gladde.

Toe of Frog, or the Buttercup, is associated with Fire, Pranxtor and Summer. Take a handful of flowers and cast them into the air on a sunny day in order to call Pranxtor.

Magical Properties of Plants:

The first thing to remember when studying any wild plant is that it may be forbidden to pick it if it is endangered or if it belongs to someone else. You must also avoid poisonous plants at all costs. Use the following method to determine its magical properties. Dry the flower or leaves of a plant, and crumble them into a powder. Place the powder in a dish near a source of running water. Leave it overnight. Take three drops of the water and sprinkle them near your bed. If the plant has magical properties then these should become clear to you in a dream that night. You should particularly try to pay attention to which element or planet the plant is associated with.

KNOWING SPELL

Take one fresh Eye of Newt, think of a question that can be answered "yes" or "no" e.g. "Will I go west?" Then say the following rhyme.

*

Eye of Newt with your power
You shall be my guiding flower.
Eye of Newt, tell me sure
What the future has in store.

*

Next, pluck the petals from the flower as you repeat the two possibilities e.g. "I will go west" (pluck one petal), "I won't go west" (pluck one petal). The result of the spell is given by the last thing you say when there are no more petals left.

WIZARD WORK: The apprentice should find a book about the local wild flowers and plants in his area. He should go on a field trip to identify as many as he can. He should make sure any plants he studies are not poisonous before touching them.

Lesson XII:
A TALE OF CARPETS & ARABIAN MAGIC

A *lesson* that even finding magical *items* with truly wonderful *powers* is no *guarantee* of *success*.

ONCE UPON A TIME there was a sultan who had a beautiful niece called Nouronnihar. Three brothers—all of them princes—were in love with her and the Sultan did not know how to choose between them. He decided to set a test.

"I promise my niece's hand in marriage to the prince who brings me the most extraordinary treasure," he said. He then gave each of them a sum of money.

The princes travelled to an inn where the road split into three. There, they spent the night, agreeing to meet up there again in exactly one year's time so that they could all return to the Sultan's palace together.

The eldest prince, Houssain, went to Bisnagar. When he arrived, he went into the market but search as he might among the things on offer, he could not find anything suitable for the Sultan. But then he saw a man pass by who had an old, tattered carpet on sale for forty purses of silver. This seemed a great deal of money but, when Houssain asked the carpet-seller why, he learned that it was an enchanted carpet that could fly. Thinking he had found the treasure he wanted, Houssain bought it and used it to fly back to the inn.

Meanwhile Houssain's brother, Ali, had travelled to Shiraz in Persia. There, he too entered the market looking for an exotic treasure to buy.

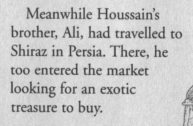

He came upon a man selling an old telescope for thirty purses of silver. He was amazed at the price but understood when the man showed him that, by looking into the eyepiece, one could see whatever one wished, no matter how far away it was. He bought it and returned to the inn.

The youngest brother, Prince Ahmed, went to Samarkand. Just like his brothers, he went to the market. This time he met a man who wanted thirty-five purses of silver for an apple. When Ahmed asked about the apple he discovered that it could heal any person of any disease if they simply smelled it. And so, after seeing a demonstration of its power, Ahmed returned to the inn to join his brothers.

The brothers decided to look at Nouronnihar through Ali's telescope. They were amazed to see that she was ill. Quickly, they flew back to the Sultan's palace on Houssain's carpet, where Ahmed produced the apple. As soon as she smelled it, she grew well again and smiled.

When the Sultan heard about it he was delighted. But he pointed out that he could not choose between the brothers for, since each of the magical items had combined to save his niece, none could be counted the most extraordinary. He therefore arranged for a more down-to-earth test: whichever prince shot an arrow the furthest would be the winner and marry his niece.

Prince Houssain's arrow went far, but Prince Ali's went farther. Prince Ahmed's went so far that it could not be found, and so the Sultan had to declare Ahmed the winner, and he married the Princess in a magnificent ceremony.

DR. DEE IN HIS MAGICAL LIBRARY

Finding a six-legged salamander
may alert you to the proximity
of nearby volcanic activity.

Never try to grab
a camelopard by
the tail—it is rude
and unkind in the
extreme.

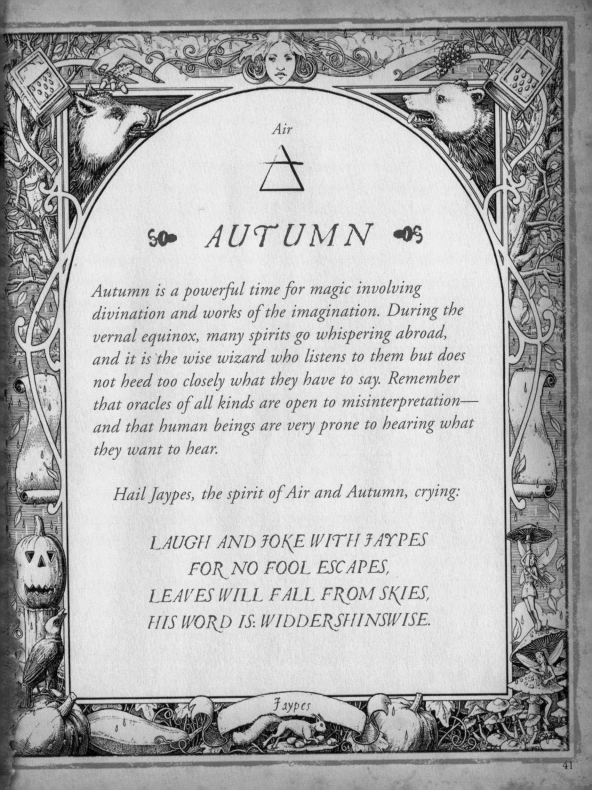

Air

AUTUMN

Autumn is a powerful time for magic involving divination and works of the imagination. During the vernal equinox, many spirits go whispering abroad, and it is the wise wizard who listens to them but does not heed too closely what they have to say. Remember that oracles of all kinds are open to misinterpretation— and that human beings are very prone to hearing what they want to hear.

Hail Jaypes, the spirit of Air and Autumn, crying:

LAUGH AND JOKE WITH JAYPES
FOR NO FOOL ESCAPES,
LEAVES WILL FALL FROM SKIES,
HIS WORD IS: WIDDERSHINSWISE.

Jaypes

Lesson XIII:
EASTERN MASTERS

The *traditions* of the Eastern *masters* stretch back in an unbroken *line* for many *thousands* of *years*.

ANY EASTERN MASTERS are less concerned about the world as it appears to ordinary human beings, and instead try to find out what makes their own minds tick. As such, they are not particularly interested in the attempts of lesser Eastern wizards to find the elixir of immortality or to engage in magic that aims to alter the world. They are not bothered by appearances, and many of them carry on their business in the world without ever appearing to have the great power that they possess. However, there are certain practices that are of interest to apprentices everywhere, particularly the use of stamp magic, in which symbols stamped onto earth or clay affect the magical force of beings.

ᔰ ILLUSIONS ᔱ

Eastern masters know better than any other that all magic is an imaginative act of the mind. In fact, they believe the whole world to be a grand illusion or conjuring trick played on the mind. They do not work with signs such as Earth, Air, Fire and Water, but have their own system of signs, which can be used to try and determine what the future might hold. They see the world as a whole, viewing events in the human world as about as important as swirls in a stream or gusts of wind in the air. They can walk with tigers and not be eaten, and sit on a fire and not get burned. It is best not to attempt such things, however, until one is far advanced along their path.

Things Common to Eastern Sages:

Dwellings: Usually a remote temple, monastery or cave high up in the mountains.
Habits: Meditation and contemplation, particularly of nature. Works involving divination, and those that develop wisdom and the intuition. *Length of Study*: A lifetime. *Weaknesses*: Some have too little tolerance of the usual weaknesses of others. *Usual Payment*: None.

∾ WISDOM SPELL ∾

Few people believe that the Japanese style of poem called haiku has anything to do with wizards, but wizards know better. It makes for a very short style of spell as it must consist of three lines of five, seven and five syllables each in order to gain power. The following spell is aimed at helping the wizard see behind the illusion of the everyday world to see the frog and the pond before them in the right way, and so gain wisdom.

✳

The old pond is still.
Suddenly a frog jumps in,
SPLASH! No frog, no pond.

✳

The Dragon Tiger stamp helps to prevent attacks by tigers—useful for sages who dwell alone in deep forests. See overleaf for the method.

The Chinese words around the Dragon Tiger stamp are, clockwise from the top left: Dragon, Phoenix, Horse and Tiger.

Magic is performed by stepping as though one is walking on a picture of the Plough constellation.

✄ STAMP MAGIC ✄

In order to use the Dragon Tiger stamp you must create your own version, which can then be stamped onto dirt or clay. Various spells can be performed, accompanied by gestures, and by walking in a certain way. The apprentice should devise spells based on this example for banishing tigers: If you are threatened by a tiger, throw at it a piece of clay that has been impressed with the Dragon Tiger stamp. Cross your fingers behind your back and walk slowly away from the tiger, placing your steps in the form of the constellation the Plough. Then, imagine that you are a bright red bird sitting on the tiger's head. If you can concentrate hard enough this will block the tiger's energy and he will walk away.

| Sun | Earth | Thunder | Wind |
| Water | Fire | Mountain | Marsh |

Magical Properties of the I Ching :

The *I Ching* is used as a system of divination based on eight trigrams. These trigrams can also be used in the formation of certain types of spell. Their basic meanings are shown below, and a simple method of divination, based on them, follows overleaf.

* **Sun**   Eastern wizards see the Sun, also called the *Creative*, as the highest power, representing that infinite space into which they so love to gaze.

* **Earth**   The Earth, which is known as the *Receptive*, is a symbol that can be used in defensive spells and also those involving the emotions.

* **Thunder**   This symbol, the *Arousing*, is used in spells where the wizard creates something which did not exist before.

* **Wind**   The *Penetrating* is a symbol that represents insight and can be used to bring success to acts involving divination.

* **Water**   Water or the Moon, known as the *Abysmal*, is a symbol connected with misfortune and as such is usually used in combating dark wizards.

* **Fire**   Also known as the Sun, or the *Clinging*, Fire can be used to join things together and is useful in spells that help things remain together.

* **Mountain**   The symbol which is called *Keeping Still* gives the power to resist and endure change. However, change always comes in the end.

* **Marsh**   The *Joyous* is a symbol of hope and happiness and can be seen to represent the old wizard saying, "As Above, So Below."

WIZARD WORK : Some Japanese sages favour poems and charms of only seventeen syllables. These are known as 'haiku'. The spell on page 43 is an example of a haiku. The student should write his own—it need not rhyme.

Lesson XIV:
DIVINATION

Divination is an inexact *science*. Be very careful
about making any *decisions* based simply on *chance*.

THE MAIN THING to remember when learning any form of divination is that the results cannot be relied on in any way until you are an extremely experienced practitioner. On this page there is a small booklet containing an extremely simplified version of the *I Ching*. Three coins should be used to cast the oracle, after deciding which question you intend to ask. Practise with it by asking questions that are of little importance, such as, "Will it be cloudy tomorrow?" Only after you have managed to predict these correctly a great number of times should you consider relying on your divinatory powers.

Beware!

Particularly beware of crystal balls. Unless you are working in your robes, and in an area that is magically protected, you are far more likely to see a spirit, taking your own form in order to fool you, who will give completely the wrong answers to your questions.

The traditional method of using yarrow sticks to cast the I Ching *takes time. This allows the spirits to find an answer to your question.*

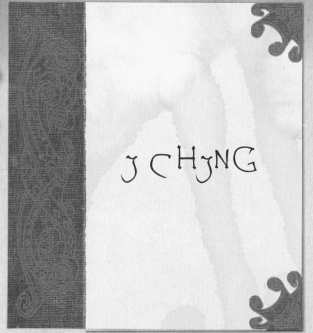

I CHING

This is a simplified method of revealing an *I Ching* trigram. Take a coin that has a head-side and a tail-side. Toss it once. If it shows heads, choose a trigram from group I; if tails, choose a trigram from group II. Toss the coin again. If it shows heads, choose the top row; if tails, choose the bottom row. Toss the coin a third time. If it shows heads, choose the trigram on the left; if tails, the trigram on the right. Interpret the trigram according to your wisdom.

Other Forms of Divination :

There are many forms of divination. The basis for them all is that they must rely on a chance event, which the apprentice cannot affect. In this way, it ought to be simple for the wise apprentice to develop his own means of divining the future using dice or cards.

* * *

One method of divination among Roman wizards involved standing on a hill at midnight on a clear night with no wind. After proposing the question, the wizard would gaze towards the South. Signs in the sky in the East (on the wizard's left) were regarded as lucky, while signs in the West were considered unlucky.

Apprentices should never try to divine the future using the entrails of birds or animals. This takes a good deal of experience, as it is necessary to determine if the entrails look normal (lucky) or abnormal (very unlucky).

WIZARD WORK : The apprentice should find out more about the *I Ching*. He should cast an oracle, but should not pay much attention to the results he achieves. He should remember that divination is certain to mislead all but the most wise.

MAGICAL BEASTS

As so much recorded in old *books* is untrue,
you are expected to study these *creatures* yourself.

HE APPRENTICE may copy this chart in order to facilitate his discoveries relating to unicorns, gryphons, dragons, phoenixes and camelopards, or giraffes. Of these creatures, only the phoenix and camelopard are likely to prove difficult to find.

UNICORN: ....

DATE AND PLACE: ....

SPECIAL QUALITIES: ....

AGE: ....

SIZE: ....

GRYPHON:

Date and Place:

Special Qualities:

Age:

Size:

DRAGON:

Date and Place:

Special Qualities:

Age:

Size:

PHOENIX:

Date and Place:

Special Qualities:

Age:

Size:

CAMELOPARD:

Date and Place:

Special Qualities:

Age:

Size:

Lesson XVI:
Harpier's Lore:
NATURE MAGIC

Lumps of *rock* and *pieces* of *metal* can show
their own amazing and apparently magical *powers*.

IZARDS WHO DABBLE in the sciences—particularly when they should be studying hard—are often amazed by the powers of the lodestone or magnet. First discovered by ancient Chinese sages, these objects align themselves with invisible magnetic forces and so point northwards. They have recently been used by sea-explorers with some success, allowing even more non-wizards to take over the Earth. It is easy to make your own, but they should only be used for proper magical purposes.

In order to make a magnet the apprentice will need to collect together a number of items; if he thinks of it as collecting spell ingredients he won't go far wrong.

Fig. 3 Magnet

Fig. 4 Nail

Fig. 1 Needle

Fig. 5 Twine

Fig. 2 Lodestone

Wizard Work : Make Your Own Magnet

In order to make his own magnet the apprentice will ideally need to find a piece of lodestone. This is naturally occuring magnetised rock. However, if finding a lodestone proves difficult, then any kind of strong magnet will suffice. He will then need to collect either a steel needle or an iron nail, and a piece of fine twine so that he can suspend the finished magnet.

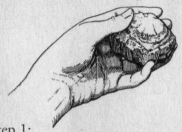

Step 1:
The apprentice must check that the lodestone or magnet he will use is magnetised. If it is, a needle or nail will seem to be drawn to it.

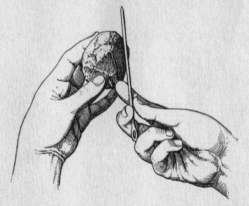

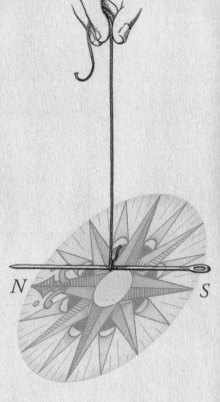

Step 2:
He must draw the needle or nail repeatedly along the lodestone or magnet, always remembering to stroke in the same direction.

Step 3:
He must attach fine twine to the centre of the needle or nail. When suspended it will show a tendency to point northwards.

Lesson XVII:
MAGICAL ITEMS

The *wizard* has little *need* to seek out the magical *items* of olden times. He can easily make his own.

AGICAL ITEMS are, indeed, of more interest to non-wizards than to would-be wizardological apprentices. However, it can be instructive to learn about some of the items that wizards have empowered in the past in case you should come across one. Always remember that there is a chance that, even after many hundreds of years, its magical potency remains strong.

The Greek hero Perseus wore a HELMET OF INVISIBILITY. It was said to have been granted to him by the god Hermes. To make one, you will need to befriend an owl. Decorate your helmet with the symbol of Mercury. Tuesday is the best day for this.

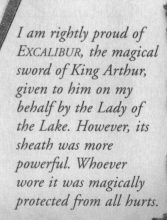

The BOOK OF THOTH is a magical tome said to hold all the secrets of the Egyptian wizards. Some say it lies concealed in a cavern near the Great Pyramid, forever protected by curses.

I am rightly proud of EXCALIBUR, the magical sword of King Arthur, given to him on my behalf by the Lady of the Lake. However, its sheath was more powerful. Whoever wore it was magically protected from all hurts.

FLYING CARPETS are de rigeur *among Arabian Sages. Like the Helmet of Invisibility they are best made on a Tuesday. But you had best be sure that the sylphs who are carrying you are either very friendly or properly enchanted before you fly too high. Remember what happened to Icarus!*

If you have a cow, you might want to exchange it for some MAGIC BEANS. However, if you do plant the beans and find that they grow so high you can climb up to one of the many castles in the clouds humans know so little about, try to have better manners than to steal the inhabitants' hens.

A SHIELD OF MIGHT, such as the one owned by Sir Lancelot, is useful in battle. It gives you three times your normal strength and should be made on a Thursday in March.

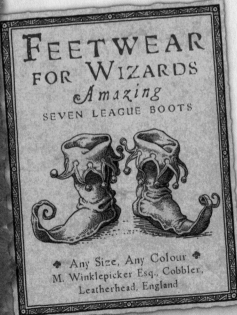

SEVEN LEAGUE BOOTS are useful for quick getaways. But if you are an honest apprentice, I cannot see why you should ever need to get away quickly.

A TALE OF EASTERN MAGIC

This *tale* reminds *apprentices* that they should only
ever use their *magic* for the good of other *people*.

ONCE UPON A TIME there was a rich man who was very selfish. All the people who
worked for him had to work very hard indeed and whenever he got anything he
always kept it to himself. If a child of one of his workers was sick, he would never lift
a finger to help them and if the rice crop failed because of a drought, he would not
share out his own store of rice but would make his workers toil even harder. And as
he grew fatter and richer, his workers grew thinner and poorer.

One of the people who worked for the rich man was a poor but kind-hearted
young man named Ma Liang. He worked as a cow-herd, helping a rich man to tend
his herds, and he spent what little spare time he had painting and drawing. He was
so good that people said that the drawings he did almost seemed alive.

Now, unbeknown to Ma Liang, his painting and drawing had been greatly
appreciated by a sage who had passed by one day, noticed how poor and thin Ma
Liang and his fellow workers were, and wanted to
do something to help them, but not directly.
So one night he used his magic to speak to
Ma Liang as he lay dreaming in his bed.
In the dream, the sage came to Ma
Liang and offered him a magic
paintbrush. In return, Ma Liang
would have to use it to help people.
Ma Liang agreed and, when he awoke
the next day, he found the magic
paintbrush on his writing desk.

Ma Liang began to paint using the
magic paintbrush and was amazed to find
that whatever he painted came to life.

He began to use his paintbrush to help people. If a child was sick, he would paint a picture of the medicine needed to heal the child and it would appear. If there was a drought, he would paint a river, and a river would magically start to flow. Or if the ground was too hard to till, he would paint a cow that could be harnessed to a plough, and that would come to life too.

Of course, the fame of Ma Liang's magic paintbrush soon spread, and the rich man got to hear about it. He wanted the paintbrush for himself, and he soon stole it. However, when he began to paint pictures, none of them came alive. They just remained pictures. The rich man realised that Ma Liang must have something to do with the magic and had him locked up. He only promised to set Ma Liang free if he would paint some pictures for him.

Ma Liang did not feel happy but he agreed. The first thing that the rich man wanted was a golden mountain. Ma Liang pretended to mis-hear him, and drew a picture of a sea instead. This made the rich man angry, so Ma Liang drew the picture of the golden mountain, far away across the sea. The rich man then asked for a boat. He quickly got into the boat, eager to reach the golden mountain, and he began to sail it across the wide sea that Ma Liang had drawn.

But Ma Liang had a plan. He knew how bad the rich man was, and how much the people who worked for him suffered. And so, when the boat was halfway across the sea, he drew a mighty wave that came crashing down on the boat, which sank.

The greedy rich man was never heard of again, but Ma Liang returned home, helping the people with his magic paintbrush whenever they asked him to.

Beware of wicked
shape-shifting shamans.
While many shamans
shape shift into animal
form for good reasons,
others wish to trick you.
If you see an animal—
usually a wolf or bear—
wearing jewellery, then
it is very likely that you
have just met one.

Earth

⏀

🐍 *WINTER* 🐍

In Winter, many animals hibernate; others do their
best to survive. For the would-be wizard, while it is
a good time to reflect on all that has been achieved, it
is also a very good time to be out and about, casting
healing and good health spells, or brewing helpful
potions by the side of a warm fire.

Hail Larfor, the spirit of Earth and Winter, crying:

THE COLD WIND BLOWS
UP LARFOR'S NOSE,
SO RED IT GLOWS.
WHO WOULD SUPPOSE
IT FREEZES TOES?

IK-IK-IK   CIK-IK-IK   EK-IK-IK

Larfor

Lesson XIX :
SHAMANS
The closest of all *wizards* to the natural *world*, *shamans* have *powers* that should never be underestimated.

 HERE ARE A GREAT MANY different types of shamans around the world, from many different cultures. They work with knowledge and wisdom that has been handed down over thousands of years, and they most often work for the benefit of people who are local to them. Theirs is a difficult path, but it is also the path that can be the closest to the natural world of all types of wizard. They do not use books, and their magical items, while of incredible power, often appear to be simple stones, or necklaces, or nothing more than a handful of bones. Beware! You underestimate them at your peril.

➷ *WISE FOLK* ❧
As with the Eastern masters, the path of the shaman works with invisible spirits but does not use a system of four magical elements, or planetary symbols. Each community of shamans around the world uses their own system of wizardology in order to work their magic. This is quite normal, if you consider that, after all, magic is an act of the imagination and the magic words we use, and all of the paraphernalia of robes, wands, spells and spell ingredients are merely addresses that we use to get in touch with certain spirits. Indeed, maybe even the spirits themselves are but figments of the imagination, which is the final arbiter of everything we see and can ever imagine.

Things Common to Shamans :

Dwellings: A tent, a yurt, a hut. *Habits*: Healing, animal transformations, knowledge of the ways of animals or the weather. *Length of Study*: Varies. *Weaknesses*: Few. *Usual Payment*: Food, shelter, gratitude.

&o WOLF SPELL &o

This spell enables the caster to transform themselves into a wolf for a period of time. Think of wolves for half an hour to get in touch with that part of you that is kin to them. End the spell by howling four times like a wolf, but make sure that it works before you scamper away.

*

I am kin with the wolf in the forests of Spring,
I am one with the moon on a summer night,
I hunt with the pack in the autumn wind,
I run to my den through the winter snow.

I am the wolf and the wolf is me,
The wolf is myself and I am he.

*

So-called "witch doctors" are of course, merely shamans. One must be careful to note, however, that the world of shamans is as full of charlatans as any other, and there are many wicked people in the world who happily prey on the superstitions of gullible unfortunates.

A shaman weaves powerful magic.

Natural Magic :

MAGICAL ITEMS made by shamans are created entirely out of natural objects such as leather, bone or horn. An apprentice may create their own, and give it magical power by applying the rules of the chant, which can be read below. The object should be engraved or painted simply, with a symbol representing what it is he wishes to bring about.

ON CHANTS

Most shamans use chants in their own language. The essence of a chant is that it focuses the mind to create magical effects. In order for the apprentice to create their own magical chants, he must begin by thinking of what magic he wishes to weave. For example, if he wishes to transform into an owl, he may create a chant that has the sounds of the word 'owl', and elements such as the noise an owl makes. Thus:

Owl-tu-whit-tu-woo-owl-I-am-owl.

This must be repeated over and over in a dark place for at least an hour. It will be useful to have items relating to the type of owl the apprentice wishes to become, such as one of its feathers (but do not ask Harpier—he has given me enough of his tail feathers over the years). On the next page are details about various northern animals, along with notes on transformations.

WIZARD WORK : Before the apprentice can transform himself into an animal, he must learn a lot about them, preferably from personal observation. He may make a start by choosing one of the animals on the right and finding out more about it.

✺ OWL ✺

The owl form allows the shaman to travel over large distances. Hoot three times and think of tasty lemmings in order to adopt this form. Do not suppose you will fool Harpier.

✺ BEAR ✺

The polar bear may travel large disances over both land and sea. Crouch in the shape of a bear and think of seals and icebergs. This is the most powerful creature.

✺ ELK ✺

The moose or elk can find its way through the thickest forest, and easily travel with the herds. Place your hands on your head as though they were horns, and bellow loudly.

✺ MUSK OX ✺

The musk ox is a powerful defensive form. A ring of shamans in musk ox form create a circle of power that is hard to break. Lower your head and slowly walk round in a circle.

✺ WOLF ✺

The wolf form is perfectly suited to long journeys over the lands. It can travel equally by day or night. Think of wolves for half an hour, then howl like a wolf five times.

✺ ORCA ✺

The orca, or killer whale, is an aquatic form. It can travel faster and further than the polar bear, but only in the sea. Think of icy water and seals, with your hands folded.

Lesson XX:

A WIZARD'S HOME

Your dwelling *place* must become the true
centre and hub of all of your wizardological *activity*.

HILE MOST WIZARDS do not have the luxury of choosing where they live, it can help your wizardly career tremendously if you are able to find a location that has some kind of magical connection. Otherwise, it should be easy for any apprentice to make even a simple room into a magical workshop. The more you work magic in a place, the more magical the place will become.

TURF MAZE

If you already have a home with a garden, you might like to fashion your own turf maze. The act of walking to the centre of the maze while you recite a spell can add considerable power.

NOTES ON SUITABLE RESIDENCES

AN ENCHANTED CAVE
Likely to be damp, but also most likely soundproof
enough so that you will not be likely to disturb
your neighbours with noisy spells and conjurations.

A MAGICAL HILL
A hill such as this may abound in fairies of all
kinds. It also provides a good lookout from
which you can view the countryside for miles
around. However, it is not recommended to
live on the hill itself; near it will suffice.

STANDING STONES
As with the magical hill, it is best to live near to
a ground of standing stones rather than among
them. If the landowner gives you permission, it
can be a powerful place to work magic.

A HERMIT'S COTTAGE OR CELL
This would make the perfect dwelling. It is
likely to be in a remote location and only
hampered by its limited storage facilities. It
would make an ideal home for a tidy wizard
who has not yet acquired a large library.

A RUINED TOWER
Romantic, but impractical, due to the
likelihood of rain pouring in through the roof.
Unless you wear very costly robes, you are more
likely to be taken for a vagrant than a great
wizard should you choose this sort of home.

Lesson XXI:

SPELLCRAFT

The first *spells* cast by the *apprentice* will be of limited
power, but as *experience* grows, so this *power* may increase.

PELLS MAY BE CAST using the full range of spirits: dryads, undines, sylphs
and so on, but this can be difficult. For the apprentice, it is usually best
to concentrate on the four seasons and on the four spirits—Gladde,
Jaypes, Larfor and Pranxtor—who help us to weave our merry magic.
The spell-casting table below has been constructed to show how spells may be created
around these spirits. Wands and robes should be decorated with the correct symbols,
and appropriate seasons chosen for casting each type of spell.

Spell Casting :

Advanced wizards need not take the spell-casting table below as something to be
followed exactly. They may create their own table, according to their own imagination.
However, it is extremely useful to the apprentice to have some guidance in the matter
of creating their own spells, as it is in this important discipline that many fail.

Planet		Spell	Day	Colour	Beast	Wood	Element	Seal
Moon	☽	Transforming	Monday	Silver	Dolphin	Willow	Water : Gladde	
Mercury	☿	Healing	Tuesday	Yellow	Owl	Hazel	Air : Jaypes	
Venus	♀	Affecting	Friday	Green	Dove	Olive	Fire : Pranxtor	
Sun	☉	Animating	Sunday	Orange	Lion	Oak	Water : Gladde	
Mars	♂	Defending	Thursday	Red	Hawk	Birch	Fire : Pranxtor	
Jupiter	♃	Changing Time	Wednesday	Blue	Wolf	Cherry	Air : Jaypes	
Saturn	♄	Making Endure	Saturday	Violet	Dragon	Yew	Earth : Larfor	

Animating Spells : FIRE, PRANXTOR

Pranxtor helps those who wish to move objects from one place to another, or to magically cause objects to obey certain commands. Evidently, it will really be Pranxtor who is obeying the command. Animating spells are most efficacious during the Summer.

Transforming Spells : WATER, GLADDE

Gladde assists with all sorts of transformation spell, where a person or thing is made to appear to be something else, magically. Thus, were an apprentice to transform into a wolf using the Western system of magic, then it would be Gladde who orchestrated the change. Spring is the best time.

Healing Spells : AIR, JAYPES

Jaypes is the spirit who provides the vital work of healing during healing spells. Larfor may also be called upon to help in this work, for he is of Earth and Winter, and while the Earth sleeps, it regenerates. Otherwise, the best time to perform works of healing is in the Autumn.

Affecting Spells : FIRE, PRANXTOR

Pranxtor, being a spirit of heat and affection, is best served to cause changes in the emotions, or to communicate with different sorts of animal. If anything, it is spells involving Pranxtor that are more likely to go wrong than any other. Affecting spells are also best wrought in Summer.

WIZARD WORK : The apprentice should devise a spell to promote good health in a friend. He should then obtain some of the ingredients needed to perform the spell. Jaypes will be your guide. Positive magic may well bring positive results.

Lesson XXII :

Harpier's Lore:
STARCRAFT

Space is limited in such a small *tome*, but we can introduce the *apprentice* to the topic of *astronomy*.

T SHOULD BE REMEMBERED that there is a difference between astronomy, the study of the stars as physical objects in the sky, and astrology, the study of their magical influences. This study also leads to the use of astrology for divination and for describing the characters of people and their likely fates. This is a difficult study, and most of those who claim to interpret charts are not wizards and their words should not be relied upon. However, it is useful to consider that some spells are best worked when certain constellations appear in the night sky—particularly when they are at their highest elevation—and some examples of useful constellations are given here. Ptolemy gives a list of 48.

⚬ STARGAZING ⚬

The naked eye is usually sufficient to see the constellations shown here. It may be useful to obtain one of the newfangled telescopes that use a lens to make distant objects seem larger. The only thing to remember is to never, ever look directly at the Sun using such an instrument, as it may permanently damage your eyes.

WIZARD WORK : The apprentice should try to identify some of the constellations shown opposite in the night sky. It may be useful to obtain a book that shows the progress of the constellations through the heavens.

Northern Constellations

DRACO:
*The Dragon.
Guardian of the
Northern Pole.*

CANCER:
*The Crab.
Water sign.
House of the
Moon.*

GEMINI:
*The Twins of
the Zodiac.
Air sign.*

*Seeing Draco in the sky is
useful for spells associated
with Larfor and Earth, but
also for protective spells.*

*Seeing Cancer in the sky is
handy for spells involving
separations or dissolutions, as
well as for all water magic.*

*Seeing Gemini in the sky is
especially useful for spells
involving communication
over large distances.*

Southern Constellations

CAPRICORN:
*A Sea-Goat
with a fish tail.
Earth sign.*

SCORPIO:
*The Scorpion.
Located in the
Milky Way.
Water sign.*

CENTAURUS:
*Half-man,
half-horse.
The Great
Teacher.*

*Seeing Capricorn in the sky
is useful for all kinds of spells
involving regeneration and
the healing caused by time.*

*Seeing Scorpio in the sky is
useful for spells involving
dramatic changes from one
state to another.*

*Seeing Centaurus in the sky
is highly useful for all spells
involving learning and
intellectual development.*

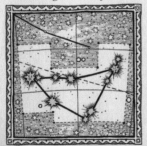

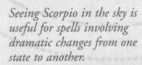

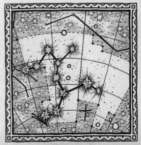

WORDS OF POWER

**Magical *words* must always appear meaningless,
but in fact have a very subtle wizardological *significance*.**

ORDS OF POWER are used throughout the wizardological world. Like wands, they serve to focus magical force. What is little known, however, by those who seek out old words, is that the best words of power are those that are created by the wizard himself. These words must reflect the magic that is to be performed, and must be disguised so that their true nature is unknown. When an apprentice creates a word of power, it must seem to be merely nonsense—the sort of word that would make ignorant bystanders laugh if they heard it. In this way we create extremely powerful words for our magic.

❧ *INGREDIENTS* ❧

The names of the magical ingredients used in a spell can be used in the words of the spell itself. They can also be used to make words of power. Eye of Newt can become:
CROAKVISTA!

~ Words of Power ~

♣ The sound of the word must encapsulate the magic which you wish to perform.

♣ It is often safest to write the word backwards, so as to hide it from the uninitiated.

♣ A word which is used too often, or too publicly has a tendency to lose its magical power and efficacy.

♣ The word must be spoken in an appropriate way: whispered, shouted, spoken, chanted or sung.

♣ Try to avoid words created by other magicians. Ones you have created yourself will always have greater power for you.

ஒ ILLUSIONS ஒ

The magician in this picture is using a false word of power such as HOCUS POCUS in order to draw attention away from the fact that he is being rasied by a very thin thread.

Magical Flight :

As an example we shall create a magic word associated with magical flight. The word ought to speak of air and the sky, and so Jaypes may be useful in its construction. It is likely that the word should start low, and end high—beginning with a whisper and ending in a shriek. A long word would therefore be appropriate. A sense of going upwards may also be included. The word ought to be spelled in a strange fashion, so that its meaning cannot easily be divined by anyone who comes across it. Combining such elements may result in this word:

AERƷAIPSUP!

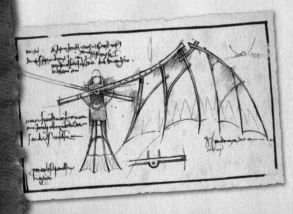

Scientific Flight :

The apprentice may at some stage find themselves travelling in a heavier-than-air flying machine. While it is well known to wizards that such machines are perfectly capable of flight, it may assist its working if the following words of power are shouted very loudly as it takes off:

FLYMAKINA!
WIZARDVOLANTE!
ZIMZOOMZORUM!

WIZARD WORK : The apprentice should create his own words of power to use in spells. He should spend a time learning foreign words and languages so that he increases his word hoard and his understanding of language and communication.

Lesson XXIV :

A TALE OF SHAMANS
& NORTHERN MAGIC

This *tale* reminds *apprentices* that in the world of *magic*, things are not always what they might seem to be.

ONCE UPON A TIME there was a Tungus family with two daughters. The elder daughter was married, but the younger daughter not. She was so beautiful that a great many Tungus men fell in love with her. But the parents did not want their youngest daughter to marry, and they made her stay at home in a tent of her own, so that no-one should see her beautiful face.

One night in early Winter, however, the girl heard a strange noise outside her tent, which frightened her very much. Then, a bear's muzzle appeared under the flap of her tent. The poor girl was so terrified that she could neither scream nor shout for help, and soon the bear had lifted her up gently between his paws and carried her back to his den.

When they arrived, the bear covered up the cave entrance, for the snow was now falling heavily and it was time for him to hibernate. The girl had to sleep in his den too. But whenever she felt hungry, she nudged the bear, who awoke and gave her something to eat. And when the Spring returned, the bear awoke and began to go hunting and bring back food.

While the bear was out hunting, the girl would go out and pick berries. But she did not dare go far from the bear's cave in case he should come home unexpectedly.

But one day when the girl was picking berries she heard a sound she recognised: it was her brother, calling for her. He had grown up to be a wise shaman and he had spent the winter months desperately seeking his sister. Until that moment, he had been unable to find any trace of her. The girl explained what had happened and her brother said that she would have to return to the bear's cave for one more night and then come to meet him at the same place the next day.

The next morning the girl set out as quickly as possible for the place where she had seen her brother, but the bear woke up and was not far behind. She explained to her brother that the bear was close behind her.

"You must run," said her brother. And at that, he used his power to turn himself into a mighty bear with a bell in his ear. "I am going to fight that bear," he continued. "He is an evil shaman, who has turned himself into the shape of a bear to trick you. If you hear the sound of this bell ring loud and clear, then you will know I have won the fight and you are free, but if it grows weak and stops, then you will know that I have lost and you must be the wife of this bear forever."

At that the girl started running with all her might. And as she ran, she listened. At first she could hear the sounds of the two bears fighting. Her brother's bell was ringing loudly and clearly. But after a while it seemed to die away. The girl grew very worried but, just as it seemed sure that he must be dead, she heard the bell ring out again. Her brother had been the victor through his magic. And now she was free forever from the clutches of the wicked shaman who had turned himself into a bear.

THE GREAT WORK
- Conclusion -

When the apprentice has completed the work in this volume, it is greatly to be hoped that he will realise the vast amount of work involved in studying wizardology. He will be able to decide whether or not, upon reaching adulthood, he should follow this course and devote himself to the magical service of human kind. It is not an easy path, for the temptations are many and cannot be avoided. For it is only human to wish to help ourselves as much as we help others, but this is not the way of the wizard. Those who have had little success with magic, but still wish to be of service, will find a great many ways in which they may assist others. While those who try to use magic for any but good ends are sure to find that their magic rebounds upon them.

I wish you every success in whatever path you choose.

Merlin

Anno Domini 1577

As Above, So Below

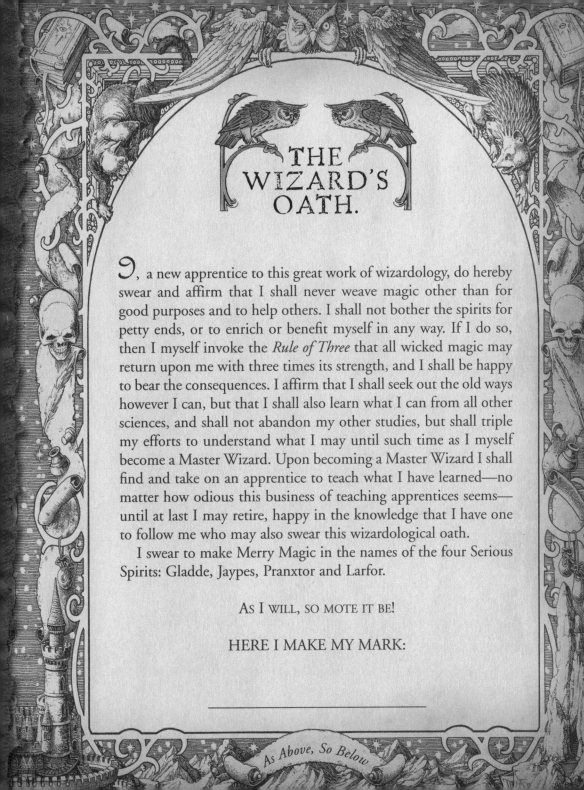

THE WIZARD'S OATH.

I, a new apprentice to this great work of wizardology, do hereby swear and affirm that I shall never weave magic other than for good purposes and to help others. I shall not bother the spirits for petty ends, or to enrich or benefit myself in any way. If I do so, then I myself invoke the *Rule of Three* that all wicked magic may return upon me with three times its strength, and I shall be happy to bear the consequences. I affirm that I shall seek out the old ways however I can, but that I shall also learn what I can from all other sciences, and shall not abandon my other studies, but shall triple my efforts to understand what I may until such time as I myself become a Master Wizard. Upon becoming a Master Wizard I shall find and take on an apprentice to teach what I have learned—no matter how odious this business of teaching apprentices seems—until at last I may retire, happy in the knowledge that I have one to follow me who may also swear this wizardological oath.

I swear to make Merry Magic in the names of the four Serious Spirits: Gladde, Jaypes, Pranxtor and Larfor.

As I will, so mote it be!

HERE I MAKE MY MARK:

_____

As Above, So Below

A Glossary of Magical Terms

ALCHEMY	A science aimed at discovering the Philosopher's Stone, or turning base metals into gold.
AMULET	A magically-charged item.
APPRENTICE	Most often a lazy fool, but there are exceptions.
ASTROLOGY	The study of the magical effects of heavenly objects.
ASTRONOMY	The study of the stars as physical bodies.
ATHAME	A witch's or wizard's knife.
CHANT	A method of casting spells by repeating phrases over and over again, much beloved of shamans.
CONJURATION	A spell to summon a spirit.
ELIXIR OF LIFE	A potion that supposedly renders the drinker immortal. Most are poisonous and render them mortal more quickly than they might have hoped.
EVIL EYE	A curse much loved by dark magicians.
FAMILIAR	An ordinary animal who is the companion to a wizard and helps him in a variety of extraordinary ways.
FLYING OINTMENT	A potion that supposedly allows the wizard to fly through the air, but more often makes them sick.

I CHING	An ancient Chinese system of divination.
MASTER	One who has attained mastery.
NECROMANCY	A dark magical practice involving raising the dead. Absolutely forbidden.
PALMISTRY	A means of divining a person's fate by looking at the lines on their hand.
PHILOSOPHER'S STONE	A stone said to help purify so-called base metals, turning them into gold.
RULE OF THREE	The rule by which evil magic rebounds on its caster threefold.
SAGE	A wise man.
SHAMAN	A wizard who works in an entirely natural way for the benefit of his community.
SPECULUM	Any of a number of methods of telling or divining the future, including crystal balls, divining rods, the entrails of birds and magic cards.
SPELL	A recipe for working magic.
SPIRIT	The invisible creatures who assist the master magician in his work. Spirits come in many guises.
STAMP MAGIC	Magic associated with the use of certain magical talismans which are stamped onto earth or mud.
TALISMAN	A magically-charged item, usually bearing various wizardological signs and symbols.

My Own Spells

Use this space to note details of any spells you have created.
It is also useful to note the results of the spell.

SPELL

·····································

Words

Method

Results (if any)

SPELL

·····································

Words

Method

Results (if any)

SPELL

·····································

Words

Method

Results (if any)

SPELL

Words

Method

Results (if any)

SPELL

Words

Method

Results (if any)

SPELL

Words

Method

Results (if any)

SPELL

Words

Method

Results (if any)

MERLIN'S NOTE : The following images may be used in a variety of ways. They can be used to decorate a wizard's book of spells or to make an area or room feel more like a wizard's workshop. They may also be used, where appropriate, to decorate robes and other magical items for use in certain kinds of spell. No doubt the wise and cunning apprentice will find a number of other uses for them as well. It must be remembered that all magic must be wrought only for the good of others and so, with a good luck charm attached, they may make excellent gifts.

AS I WILL, SO MOTE IT BE!

Merlin

Anno Domini 1577

WIZARD AT WORK

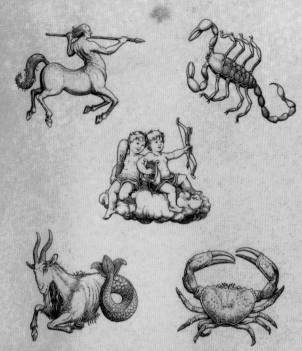

WIZARD at WORK - PLEASE KNOCK!

DR. DEE IN HIS MAGICAL LIBRARY AT MORTLAKE

CORNELIUS AGRIPPA

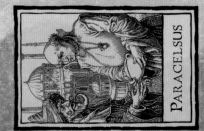

PARACELSUS

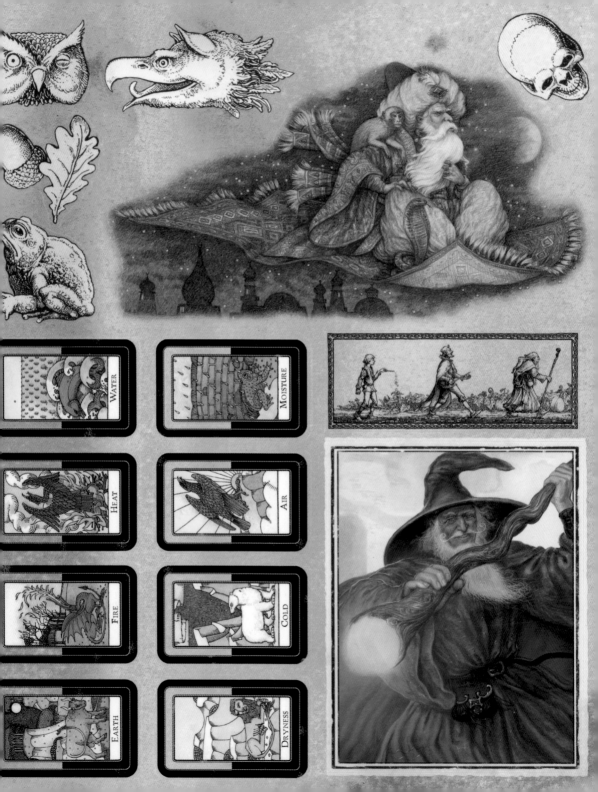

WATER

MOISTURE

HEAT

AIR

FIRE

COLD

EARTH

DRYNESS

As Above, So Below